T0129894

Our Asylum
Memoir

Our Asylum Memoir

Corridors of Gloom

ZANE MURRAY

OUR ASYLUM MEMOIR
CORRIDORS OF GLOOM

iUniverse books may be ordered through booksellers or by contacting:

iUniverse
1663 Liberty Drive
Bloomington, IN 47403
www.iuniverse.com
1-800-Authors (1-800-288-4677)

Because of the dynamic nature of the Internet, any web addresses or links contained in this book may have changed since publication and may no longer be valid. The views expressed in this work are solely those of the author and do not necessarily reflect the views of the publisher, and the publisher hereby disclaims any responsibility for them.

Any people depicted in stock imagery provided by Thinkstock are models, and such images are being used for illustrative purposes only. Certain stock imagery © Thinkstock.

ISBN: 978-1-5320-2133-6 (sc)
ISBN: 978-1-5320-2134-3 (e)

Library of Congress Control Number: 2017905501

Print information available on the last page.

iUniverse rev. date: 06/26/2017

CONTENTS

a·sy·lum

[əˈsīləm]

Noun

an institution offering shelter and support to people who are mentally ill:

"he'd been committed to an asylum"

synonyms: psychiatric hospital, mental hospital, mental institution, mental asylum

[more]

madhouse, loony bin, funny farm, nuthouse, bughouse, lunatic asylum, bedlam.

This book is dedicated to the people in these poems. Most of the poems in this book reflect depression, anxiety, self-harm, or confusion—states that I have experienced. Whether you are a child or an adult, I hope that my words, these poems, help you crawl out of whatever pit you fell in.

My passion for writing and creating saved me from torment. Hopefully, you'll find your own passion or salvation through my words, my writings.

Our Asylum Memoir

Corridors of Gloom

ZANE MURRAY

LOST

- Feeling like I didn't know where I was, what I was doing; and someone, please help me …

Draw your own interpretation of these words ...

Silent Hill

Every morning I wake up 6:00 a.m.
Moon still out as if it be a clear gem.
Darkness in my room, same as the night.
This place I live just isn't right.

Outside of my head leads to the mill
That holds and stores nothing but thrill.
Mist and fog lie upon the streets.
Nothing to notice but my bloody sheets.

Monsters walk the streets during the night and during the day,
Limping and crawling on all fours; demons I must slay.
Nothing can be done because I just am so weak
No one knows me better than just a useless freak.

It's silent in this city, and I can only hear my feet clamp
On the gravel of a road that leads to another nightmare, leaving my
heart as a broken lamp,
I'm not sure what to call this place, either home or hell.
I can hear sirens going off, and then I get a whiff of this foul smell.

I'm not sure where I am—Earth or mind.
I've never realized how I, as a monster maybe, could be blind,
Wandering in my own place that no one else sees.
And if they did see it, it would give their spines a chill.
I really don't know; I just keep running from the creatures.
Maybe I'm locked in my own Silent Hill.

Draw your own interpretation of these words ...

Screaming

Day by day, in this pit of hell,
I lie there, being tormented,
Hoping someone will ring the bell
And make the pit illuminated.

My screams go out through scars.
How can no one hear me?
I'm locked in with this depression behind bars.
Can no one hear me?

For so long I've been screaming.
I try so hard to get you to see,
But I keep on bleeding,
Thinking it will never be.

Get me out of this pit.
It's dark and cold.
I'm alone and need company a bit.
I'm getting exhausted; it's getting old.

Hear my cry, loud and shredding.
Listen very closely.
It's hard to hear while dreaming.
It's just like a red herring,
So try to get comfortable and cozy.
Can you hear me screaming?

Draw your own interpretation of these words ...

Leave Me Alone, My Dear

My mind is a canvas that I make my own.
Depending on my mood, I'll let some be shown.
Showing it may be dark, and sometimes light,
But no matter what it is, it'll make a hard bite.

Beware of my impulses and mistakes I am to make.
They can be so intense, it'll make your bones shake.
I am that I am, forever more.
Don't be afraid of the blood and the gore.

When you see what I see, this war in my mind,
You'll know the reason I'm not so kind.
It goes on and on, without precious end.
It damages me so with an unbearable bend.

Depression is what I call it; it swallows me whole—
Me, myself, and I, but mostly my soul.
Don't look at my canvas with sorrow or remorse.
It will take you and I down with unstoppable force.

Look away for your own sake, please.
Keep your happiness, and live life with ease.
I wouldn't want to bury you with me here.
Acknowledge this, and leave me alone, my dear.

LONELY

- People ignoring me, leaving me, or just not caring ...

Draw your own interpretation of these words ...

Love and Pain

For all the pain that I am to feel,
I will always be able to heal.
But because of my love for you,
There really isn't any healing to do.

My heart was yours, saved in a locked box,
Held tight, and you wound its gears like a clock's.
But because of your choice to go, it has left pain,
And I won't get the chance again to kiss you every day.

I can hardly breathe; my chest is so weighted.
I took my heart back only to have it plated.
In front of your house, staring up at your window,
Waiting for you to look down at me, winning the limbo.

My sadness is back, lost grip of your hand,
Letting go when we were together by the sand.
We are still friends, but that feeling isn't the same.
Never really knew the rules of our little love game.

I need you back again; please come.
I can't get used to this feeling of being numb.
My heart is cold again, and it really stings.
But sometimes I tell myself that love and pain
Are the same things.

Draw your own interpretation of these words ...

Stone, Yet Me

My heart is stone.
No emotion seen.
Feeling the lies of society,
Of the punkers, the loners.

Showing no complexion to anyone but myself,
Blade on my bookshelf.
Tried to be cool, but it didn't work out.

With my mind in a box,
Sadder than a wounded fox,
Lying in the darkness of my room, alone with myself.
No violence, no hate, only love for my body,
Myself.
Tried to understand girls; asked the girl of my dreams out, she denied.
I went home and cut myself; I cried.

I'm not the only kid this way, making the rhyme of sticks and stones.
No, my heart is stone, with bones and marrow.
Hoping that tomorrow will be a better day
To express myself, to be one of a kind,
To find that to destroy me is to destroy them.

They called me maggot, bitch, punk, and worst of all, a faggot.
But I realize myself is the key.
I fight for a better darkness in my room.
With a little light.

Without a blade in my hand and not fading into the night.

To see that blood ooze from my cut.
It's my calm time.
But I realize there is a way out
Because my heart of stone
Is starting to heal me.
I realize it's stone, yet me.

Draw your own interpretation of these words ...

Lucy

Hmm? ...
Where am I? ...
It's so bright and warm, warmer than a bath in the cold winter ...
It's a room; I have no idea how big or small, but it's all white ... and pure ...
I can hear dripping ... the rest is just pure silence ...
I'm naked ... nothing but a sort of towel ...
No one is here; it's just ...
No ... I'm not alone ...
I turn around and see ... a tall man ...
Long, golden, and luscious hair ... in a white cape, gilded in gold ...
I'm frozen, maybe a bit scared ...
I start walking toward him ... slowly realizing there is water under my
feet ...
I splash through ... slowly making soft waves ...
I get closer to the man ... and then he reaches out his arms and says,
"Come here, my friend." ...
I am no longer hesitant ... and I start walking faster; in only the snap
of the fingers ...
I'm in his arms ...
I notice that it's warmer than the room ... and I'm wrapped around
his cape ...
His heartbeat is being skipped ... one beat every forty-five seconds ...
slow ... remedy ...
His breath is sweet, like lavender ... soft and gentle ...
Am I dreaming? ...
I pinch myself ...
"You've passed on," he says ...
"You're in the spirit realm, in which you'll dwell with me, forever ..."
"Who are you?" I ask ...
"Lucifer," he says slowly and deeply ...
He hugs me tighter ...
I can't breathe ...
Then ...
Black...

HURT, SAD, ANGRY

- Upset overall because I didn't know what to do, would pout that I didn't know, and was angry no one would help ...

Draw your own interpretation of these words ...

Detrimental Isolation

Stuck in a dream of laces and walls,
Wanting to come out and see,
See the world that we are surrounded by—
Worthless cars, worthless classes to take,
Making us smarter; no, it's getting harder to see
What will make us be without an outlet,
Leading to the world that we wish to think of and be.

Some people are stuck, can't breathe,
Can't see and hear the laughter of the people who live,
A life of joy; can't feel the vibrations of the hearts of the valiant,
Stuck in a cage of barbwire,
Too cold to bear the warmth of an escape led by a girl of marks and beauty,
Ending up at the doorstep of the faithful, to the people who free.

We are stuck; we try to see the world with our own eyes,
But the glare and stare of a screen, built by the bitterness of men,
Guide us only to fake, not allowing us to wake up,
Move to a place of more matters of happiness.
What is happiness, the feeling of new thinking?
Feeling, smelling, hearing of the things that make you glow
As bright as the stars that might fall.
The pinholes of night that seem to never meet your closet wall.

Draw your own interpretation of these words ...

Detrimental Isolation (continued)

Earth and sky, they are the same, the rock of green and blue
Is where we live to be the people that we want to see
Somewhere else, somewhere else than here.
Not a society, not a clique or group,
But to ourselves, out of the cells of darkness,
That we hold on to at the back of our minds
Only to find nothing but the suffering of our own bearings.

Isolation makes us rotten.
We've forgotten to look up at the stars that we all bear.
Balls of gas that should match the grass where we stand.
Understand our environment; no ... we want to leave, never to receive
Our old place in this world, held back by the people who birthed us.
"You can't leave," they say. "Stay and don't move in this world.
Only let it pass you by, don't explore,
Don't implore on making your way to a new civilization.
Instead, stay in your dark, suffering, your *detrimental isolation.*

Draw your own interpretation of these words ...

Thunder

Roar goes the thunder
When clouds go flash.
You feel the rattle go under,
And you know you have to dash.

Run inside; you keep hearing banging.
You love the thrill, the pikes.
Exciting it is, keeps on ganging.
Energy rolling during long-ass hikes.

Rumble, shake, spark goes the sky.
You wish to be that way, unstoppable.
Thinking this makes you hopeful when it passes by.
Nothing can touch you—powerful, fearless, unbreakable.

It's there for a reason.
I know it's dumb, but it's true.
It builds up every season,
Getting stronger, building up just for you.

Heart is thunder, zaps of shards.
Feel it go loud, strike every day.
It leaves hope and some deep marks.
If not, you only think it may.

Draw your own interpretation of these words ...

Rain

Some people say that the music of life is silence.
I couldn't agree more.
But my music is more appealing to me.
My music is the rain.

The sound soothes me, the light ambience,
Nothing beats the feeling of the
Soft, wet, fine rain.

It's as if the rain was meant for you.
That the moment of it
Was just there waiting for you, your joy,
As if the rain was a toy,
That came every fall.

The rain is as cold as my heart.
But with use, I find it warm, my calm time,
Walking the roads of puddles and streams,
Slowly, along the faded yellow line.

It goes on and on, splish-splash.
My present came, and it is lasting forever.
My joy is great and heartfelt.
When it stops, I release my soul.

Draw your own interpretation of these words ...

Black

Black is the color I wear.
Black is the color I see.
Black is what I bear.
Black is what I decree.

People upon people swallowing the halls—
All stare at me with complete awe.
Judgment is in the air and written on the walls.
With this feeling I solemnly lock my jaw.

Their eyes locked with mine,
My music blasting in my ears,
Acting like everything is totally fine,
But really, I am in tears.

I fear that I'll be left behind,
That no one will even look.
All the dark thoughts running through my mind,
And me, always hiding behind a book.

I tell you that these people are cruel,
That they only care about their social status,
That they find it funny to break every rule,
And that they don't even notice us.

I wait for the day for me to be set free—
That I might live in a day of light,
That people will not harshly judge me.
I really do hope that they just might.

<u>*DARK*</u>

- Thoughts on death, wondering if life was on the other side, or if I was stuck here and wanting to leave ...

Draw your own interpretation of these words ...

Tear Me Up

What kind of paradise am I looking for?
When I'm rich in love, and wealth I am poor,
I have all that I need here in my world,
But I act like I live in the Underworld.

My mind is so fucking empty,
But I remain to be one of the friendly,
Acting as if there is nothing wrong.
But really, my arms are my way to play this sad song.

Hurry up and tear me up.
I'm slowly waiting for death … yup.
Shred open my arms and forearms.
Please turn off my waking alarms.

I am so very lost,
Not knowing what my death will cost,
Hurting my friends and family because of my dead body.
But I don't, still urging for my mind disembodied.

Please, God, take me away.
Lead me up that heavenly stairway, I pray.
Swallow these pills, down the hatch,
Or on my wrists I leave a scratch.

Lock myself in my room, and make you wonder,
Am I alive or am I dead, matching the color of thunder?
Maybe I'm having shtup,
Or maybe I'm calling someone to tear me up.

Draw your own interpretation of these words ...

Drips

Drip, drip,
Slip, slip.

Drip, drip,
Slip, slip.

Drip, drip,
Slip, slip.

Blood goes drip, drip.
Razor goes slip, slip.
Down the white tunnel I make a trip, trip.

Show me your drips and slips,
And let the blood flow from those beautiful, luscious lips, lips.

My life is of knives and their tips, tips,
And my skin that is of rip, rips,
With the demons and their grips,
And the drips made from slips, slips.

Draw your own interpretation of these words ...

Ghost

I'm not sure if I'm a human with flesh and bone,

Or if I'm a ghost that killed myself when I was alone.

I literally cannot tell if I'm dead or alive.

Maybe I'm a cosmic vampire, taking people's energy to survive.

I've decided I am dead in some way or another.

My imprint of my old self is now buried down under.

Zane Murray: Requiescat in Pace, or rest in peace,

Buried in mud under a silk white fleece.

I as a spirit walk the hallways and corridors of the home of my peers.

Me leaving away my pains and my fears

As an invisible entity that only I can see.

As a gray ghost, maybe I set myself free.

Draw your own interpretation of these words ...

Hell

Tartarus, the eternal pit, full of fire and smoke,

Where the beast of the pit walks his ways in his infinite black cloak.

He walks with a sturdy step along the dust and bones of the righteous dead

And along the rivers of blood that run with the ultimate color red.

His name is Satan, Ruler of the Earth, King of the World, in his abode,

With the darkened skies that linger with thunder, along with a bird that had crowed.

No one dies here in this realm; only does the Lord of Darkness die into eternal rest here.

And only shall he be indestructible from the fire and the cries of fear.

As he walks in the darkness, with the smell of rotten meat and skin,

He scratches his legs and arms and runs his hand through the hair on his chin.

Up the mountain of doom and fire shall he see what he wants in his desire,

God, the Son, and Spirit, burning in the flames of the mount, and their grace drowning in the mire.

He sees all of the followers here in the pit along with them,

And he shouts out of his silver lungs the phrase that lights his necklace gem,

Draw your own interpretation of these words ...

Hell (continued)

"I dip my forefinger in the watery blood of your impotent mad redeemer, and write over his thorn-torn brow: The *true* prince of evil— the king of slaves!"

"And shall nothing be more of a pity than himself and when we spit on his grave!"

Never shall there be the right-hand path in the way of the dark realm

For we shall drift in the left path on which Satan shall hold the helm.

He takes the ship of the righteous dead and takes it toward the oblivion.

And tied to the hull are the martyrs of Christ, the women with the name Vivian.

And when he shall reach the port of the dead, and all the tears that have shed from them have fallen,

In the rain of acid and the visions of the wicked have engulfed them, and when the cages have dropped for the souls shall brawl in,

That is to be unknown and for only Satan to know the Lord of the Earth, King of the World, only for him to tell.

Only for him who dwells in his home of beauty in the eyes of followers, for its true name, in the fire, is called hell.

AFTERLIFE

- Personal description or picture of what death may be like and if there is, what I'd want it to be ...

Draw your own interpretation of these words ...

Devil

I've met the devil,
And he isn't a little red man with horns and a tail.

I've met the devil.
He's a man who has died and will make you cry,
And you ask, "Just why?"

I've met the devil.
He's the man who will bury you down.
The man of black shadows.
A man of the nightmarish crown.

I've met the devil.
He's in your sleep, not under your bed.
He's not hiding in your closet.
He's hiding in your head.

I've met the devil.
He's the one you conquer right before death.
The one that you kill and slay
Right before your last breath.

I've met the devil.
I've stared death in the face.
It took me little time to realize
That we were both in the same place.

I've met the devil.
His shadow of my reflection—
Black claws, eyes of fire,
Sharp teeth, and my blood is his desire.

I've met the devil.
He is yourself, your darkness inside.
You're his master, after all,
So open wide.

Draw your own interpretation of these words …

A Beautiful Death

So many people are scared of the inevitable end.

Maybe it's because they are convinced that they are condemned to

Hellfire that will roast and burn their souls and flesh.

Brainwashed by the words described by the king Gilgamesh.

Or some people love the aspect of being at the void

And accept that it is something that no one can avoid.

They embrace the end for it is the great abstinence.

That's why they live their lives fully in the great indulgence.

Angels and demons, or God and devils;

They think they can be taken away by either into the paradise or hell of nine levels.

But in my mind, it is the same as the ones who see it as beauty,

Something that we all must do; whether we like it or not, it's our duty.

I do not believe in a heaven or a hell, but I do believe in a place where we all connect together.

Maybe a place of all green gardens and fruit to eat, communion with one another.

A place where we all share the same memories of peace and serenity.

A place of all-powerful love by your loved ones and by your ancestors.

Draw your own interpretation of these words ...

A Beautiful Death (continued)

A place where we belong for it is the great abstinence, but it is different for everyone.

Wherever you think you're going, you'll probably show up there when all of the deeds are done.

For the mind is powerful in the eyes of the universe in which we dwell.

Either way, life is the great indulgence and death the great abstinence, so live your life well.

Do not be afraid, ever, of whatever is beyond.

It has to be better than the earth, where all life will bond.

Nothing shall pass on to that world that is without breath,

So go ahead and prepare, my friend, and take your one life to be a beautiful death.

Draw your own interpretation of these words ...

God and His Heaven

If there is a place that is up above,

It must be as soft as the silk of a glove.

White and shiny as the stars in the sky.

Sounds like a daydream created by a bearded guy.

They say God created the heaven and the earth on the first day.

I'm sorry, but I don't believe that, not ever and definitely not today.

Not really a place for me to keep in my mind.

I don't have to worry about something that I may or may not find.

There's a man in the clouds, staring down at me, and he isn't happy.

Says I can't masturbate with my manliness, can't go fappy fappy.

Tells me what to do and what I can't, staring down on my meaty body, like I'm one of a million ants.

He lives in paradise, a place of no suffering, letting no one normal in,

Telling people to stay out of his treehouse, punishing people like a doll full of pins,

Sends them to hell to burn for eternity, giving people leprosy,

And all you can really do is obey or say, "Really, dude? Seriously?"

Sits up there on his throne of fire around the angels of slavery.

Draw your own interpretation of these words ...

God and His Heaven (continued)

In the heavens of the earth, only a few angels that turned into demons really had any bravery.

He's just a bully, self-conscious of his appearance, never actually letting us see him.

Or maybe it's for our own good because he's an evil being, black, and his face full of sinister grim.

He has many names: Elohim, Jehovah, Yahweh.

They say he's righteous, but really, I say no way.

There's a limit that he just hit; I denied him when I was about eleven.

There's a better place that's after death I'm sure, but I sure wouldn't call it heaven.

Draw your own interpretation of these words ...

Halo

Most of us worship an invisible man.
I don't understand how people can.
We've never met him, earth, or sky.
All I ask is a simple, "Why?"

A man named God, somewhere in the clouds,
Created the earth, planted crowds.
With a big beard and white robe,
He is given faith around this blue globe.

Created hell for the wicked and bad.
Created heaven for the righteous and glad.
Sent his Son to die for our sins,
For all people, all different skins.

It's a good idea and good to hold.
It gives people hope, a city of gold.
In my eyes, a fairy tale for young kids,
Some tall, sandaled hippy said for his bids.

I have my ideas of life and death,
Things that happen after my last breath.
No city, no gold, no ancestors,
No sinners, no quitters, no molesters.

It's a place of all-knowing peace.
It's pitch-black, but we do not cease.
Somewhere beautiful as the Greek Calypso,
Somewhere in darkness but with our own halo.

<u>AWAKENING</u>

- Acceptance and revival from being in this state and my thoughts, _Everything is getting better._

Draw your own interpretation of these words ...

Barcode

Rumble, rumble goes the earth,
The place where we live, the blue marbled hearth,
Infested with people, everlasting disease,
Taking from the earth, pulling to cease.

We don't know it, but we all have a barcode.
Things that you have already blandly showed,
Something that someone else chose,
Not on our skin, not on our clothes.

All working for the plays of one person.
We think things will change, but really, they will worsen.
We forget that the people change things,
Not one person who bites and stings.

One day at a time, walk in the line,
Follow the shepherd, and everyone will be fine.
No you won't; you'll be led into death.
That barcode will expire; you're another waste of breath.

Robots dressed in suits, always a destination.
What about your natural presentation?
Tear off those numbers from the false abode.
Tear off those lines that represent the barcode.

Draw your own interpretation of these words ...

Machine

We all live in a world where darkness is falling.
We all live in a world where no one is calling.
We all want things that have no mental gain.
Because of our greed, we give pestilence, death, and pain.

In a world with slave drivers, telling you how to live,
In a broken society that refuses the audacity to give.
"Because I said so," the phrase of no reason.
They say they give you liberty, but it's only laws without season.

Don't listen to these people tell you what to do, what to think, and
what to feel.
They treat us like machines, lifeless.
We aren't even real.

Machine people with machine minds,
Machine hearts,
Taking your chances to live free,
Like a game of darts.

Live your life not by book or law.
You won't make it far; your life will be raw.
Be the rebel, show them you are the prestines.
Live life as people, not as machines.

<u>*EPILOGUE*</u>

Here it is: the end.

I hope while turning these pages, you basically read about yourself. And on realizing it, I hope you accept it and want to change.

This book is my expression of freedom of speech. I urge you to do the same through writing, music, or even speaking.

Instead of being hard on yourself for whatever reason, press hard on paper with a pencil, push hard on those strings or keys, and punch hard at the negative feelings you have. Believe me—there is light at the end of the dark tunnel.

Printed in the United States
By Bookmasters